THE

PORCUPINE'S

KISSES

Books by Stephen Dobyns

THE
PORCUPINE'S
KISSES

Stephen Dobyns

ILLUSTRATIONS BY

Howie Michels

PENGUIN POETS

PENGUIN BOOKS
Published by the Penguin Group
Penguin Putnam Inc., 375 Hudson Street,
New York, New York 10014, U.S.A.
Penguin Books Ltd, 80 Strand,
London WC2R 0RL, England
Penguin Books Australia Ltd, 250 Camberwell Road,
Camberwell, Victoria 3124, Australia
Penguin Books Canada Ltd, 10 Alcorn Avenue,
Toronto, Ontario, Canada M4V 3B2
Penguin Books India (P) Ltd, 11 Community Centre,
Panchsheel Park, New Delhi – 110 017, India
Penguin Books (N.Z.) Ltd, Cnr Rosedale and Airborne Roads,
Albany, Auckland, New Zealand
Penguin Books (South Africa) (Pty) Ltd, 24 Sturdee Avenue,
Rosebank, Johannesburg 2196, South Africa

Penguin Books Ltd, Registered Offices:
Harmondsworth, Middlesex, England

First published in Penguin Books 2002

1   3   5   7   9   10   8   6   4   2

Page 179 constitutes an extension of this copyright page.

CIP data available
ISBN 0 14 20.0244 5

PRINTED IN THE UNITED STATES OF AMERICA

Set in Galliard
Designed by M. Paul

FOR PETER PARRISH

PROSE POEMS AND CONSIDERATIONS

THE

PORCUPINE'S

KISSES

PART ONE

The clouds above the mountains of Mexico—how palpable they were, towering expanses of particles of water, layer upon layer of overlays of white, brighter than white as if lit from within, mountainous shapes cresting the mountains. He dreamt of being part of their vaporous solidity as they crossed the peaks, spreading their shadows over the emerald variations far beneath. Wouldn't he relinquish his solitude to join that snowy company? Then a darkening as thunderheads rose above the horizon—cumulonimbus, nimbostratus—soon a chill breeze, a few drops, then the deluge cascading over white adobe houses, cobblestone streets, thunder battering the sky as streets turned to rivers, rivers cataracts, and he still among them, swept toward the sea—nothing left to strive for or struggle against with his surrender a minor event already lost from memory.

The world seeks to erase itself; you work to make its details survive. What you love are such details.

One was born with an intonation and went searching for language.

Part of him felt more comfortable in the dark: the part that insisted on turning on the light.

If he could not find beauty, nothing else would be worth finding.

This one has sex to prove the world exists, that one gets bitten by the dog.

Beyond the length of his stride, the road remained dream.

Much of what he values, aren't they distractions between himself and what he lacks courage to value?

The seamless arguments he wove by the day, night found the flaws.

Often, in dreams, he moved through a city not found in the real world. From one dream to the next he charted its streets, the texture of its neighborhoods. From one to the next, he recalled what lay to the north or south, its subways and bus lines, until the city became the place he knew best: morning light upon the storefronts, bridges over the river, the rush of traffic on a hill through the park. But although he found the city beautiful, it wasn't unique—not like London or New York. It was just the location of his dreams. Yet its making became one of the major tasks of his life: its crowds, its rain or sunlight, its rich facades, even a piano heard through an open window, even the statues of city fathers in swallow-tailed coats, until its details and geography could fill several books—a dream city, all swept away when he departed from the other, the one we call real.

Look at this dark night: no stars, no moon. Look at this crowd of people. Do you know one better than the other?

It isn't yours till you can stand to see it break.

Repentant until he learns how to get away with it.

With his five senses he asserts the world's solidity, with language he makes it real.

The mansion of his ambition—he was a fly buzzing against its basement windows.

Only feels virtuous when seeking out the sins of others.

When I ask you for something, I ask you for everything.

Birds flock together to begin their long journey: he wonders what he has left undone.

Although in the thick of a journey, the ship in the bottle isn't going anywhere. It has already reached its destination, while the bottle itself is long past being emptied of its contents and has become an absence, the very atmosphere of the ship rushing nowhere with wind-filled sails. There is no end in sight; being is the paradox of stationary motion. And the wind that swells the sails, ruffles the whitecaps on a blue plastic sea, is the wind of the ship's creation, which blew in the workshop of its maker, whose restlessness was physical and existential, whose materials were chosen from the castoff and abandoned; and who, when he had completed his work, corked the bottle, walked out to the dirt street of his small fishing village to smoke a cigarette and gaze at the sea, which churns and plunges and goes no place.

Self-deception and his longing for transcendence: two branches on the tree of self-forgetting.

He is a whim in the brain of his resentments.

The rose is a dead hand on its way to becoming a star.

When you tell me something, I want you to be saying the words I hear, not the words you tell me.

Faces the future holding an empty cup.

This time in which you live—now it is gone. In any second you balance between memory and expectation. This is what you call life.

Ashamed to ask why, he learned to say because.

Rain against the window; who remains to remember him?

Over here he made a pile of what he had had and lost. Over there a pile of what he was owed. Then a pile of what he possessed and a pile of what he desired. After measuring them, he added a pile of what he deserved and put it beside the others. Then came the pile of what was his by rights, the pile of what he had failed to achieve, the pile of what he had been cheated out of, the pile of what had been stolen. His calculations took years. In the beginning he had had many gifts, different roads his life could take, now his calculations required all his attention—what he had, what others had, what he should have—all the oughts and might-have-beens. It made its own pile.

He tried to make his children his second chance and they too turned out badly.

As the hands infer the brain, so the brain infers the soul.

Feels most alive when he grieves.

That others praised his modesty became his greatest vanity.

His fear of weeping made him dance.

In the shifting clouds, he found the answers to his questions nearly articulated.

Kissed twice on the porch, starts choosing her bride's maids.

As his innocence diminished, so did his willingness to love.

Those brick walls in the older part of the city—the side of a warehouse plastered over with one layer of advertising after another, a century of mercantile history with one image visible through the next and another behind that so the wall formed a patchwork of contrary icons in back of which the crumbling bricks had nearly vanished. At times he felt like this, so masked by borrowed gesture, hidden motives, socially correct behavior, even plain hypocrisy, that the person concealed behind the tattered patchwork of what he saw as non-him—whatever non-him had come to mean— had lost all definition, like the building itself that once had housed a stable or storehouse or shop but now had become at best a landmark on the road to someplace else.

Hid by saying what others wished to hear.

Likes to be first with the bad news.

By not believing in evil, he became its accomplice.

When he wants to insult you, he calls it telling the truth.

Thief blames the open window.

Too rude to finish hearing your life story.

When he argues, other people's ideas show through the holes in his own.

He felt his judgments enlarged him; he grew larger when he refused to judge.

A Bach partita or one of the Goldberg Variations—for a short while he could follow them like a road. Or a solo piano piece by Bud Powell, Thelonious Monk—discordant, unexpected—jumping his attention into pleasure. A painting's shifts of line and color, whether a Rothko or Brueghel, its beauty's progress to his self-forgetting. But also the laughter of his children, how he can get lost in their faces as within a landscape. Even the variations of light upon the ocean, the way the air can change in spring, the sweet smell of the privet. These moments that lift him far from himself, what are the rest but clumsy transitions, the interruptions of envy, pride, ambition, those self-lessenings that clutter the spaces between himself and what he loves? Yet without such intrusions, these cheapenings and abatements, how would he know what is precious? As if only by being away can he be at home, as if only by being outside of himself can he ever be within himself.

Cold wind on his neck, he asks the dark who he is.

Chickens flattering the fox; feathers on the breeze by nightfall.

It's not events that make him afraid; his imagination makes him afraid.

Once again spring approaches. Birds begin their eager songs. Feel glad you can still be overswept.

Lets his anger become the locked door between his life and what he loves.

Glass makes of its fragility a virtue.

Small talent; big smile.

When no one disagreed, he felt he was being wise.

Occasionally and for what seemed no reason, he felt on the brink of tears. Surely some emotion was having its way with him, though he knew not why or what it might be. This flattered and even pleased him, leading him to think that his life was the envelope around an even greater life deep within him, which added a spark of color to an hour's lusterless unfolding. These moments of strong emotion: it was as if he were the servant of a gentleman of distinction, who at times crept to his master's wardrobe and draped himself with a silk jacket or scarf, which he paraded back and forth before his master's mirror. How he would strut for a minute or two, all the while listening for a step in the hall, as he raised an eyebrow and smirked and bowed—such was his claim to a few bright threads of borrowed splendor.

When he wanted to praise something larger than himself, he praised the violet.

Preferred the sincerity of envy to the possible insincerity of praise.

Clown puts on his face paint; banker puts on his tie.

By giving his heart to others, he hoped to keep it whole.

Howls at the moon; calls it music.

Each destination is Death's lieutenant.

Fox saves a tear for dessert.

Looking at someone else, the first thing I look for is something of myself.

He had spent his youth dreaming of romantic triumphs, a world where his successes would be envied. Although he had no actual plans, he knew that his road would be made clear and so he waited, getting by on talent and saving his genius for when his name would be called. But no call came and life went by. What had he expected, that he should be unhappy now? Only in nostalgia did he roam through the rich place he had been promised, but the dream would end and again he would be left among cold streets, full of regret and resentment. Once he had painted the world in bright colors, now he painted it gray. But it was the same world, neither brighter nor darker, and when he vanished from its surface, the world kept on as before with no memory of his footsteps or desire.

Before he could feel joy, he had to allow himself to feel foolish.

For the vulture, your breath is the garment around what is most precious.

Hoping to be happier, he chose bread. Each night he dreams of cake.

His opinions were the lumber out of which he made the box where his life was spent.

Mistakes aren't the enemy; regret is the enemy.

The suffering of my body makes me fear my death. My soul's suffering makes me long for it.

Every bad idea has a good reason.

Without his flatterers, where would be his genius?

He grew fond of his uncertainties. Their shared history, their increasing solidity—he could always depend on their companionship. And so he came to trust them more than he trusted what he loved. At first he had disliked how they doubted his every action, hampered his emotional life, but triumphs came and went, lovers drifted away, his children hurried down their several roads, yet his uncertainties remained, like a clumsy acquaintance he could always count on. They never let him down. They were ready with every suspicion. You know how it sometimes happens that after years of familiarity an association can ripen into something deeper? One night you meet in the dark and kiss—one of those sour cigarette-and whiskey-laden kisses. It's the only kiss that endures.

When he counts his blessings, he counts the evils that have happened to you.

By envying another's success, I become part of that success.

Fewer teeth than a tiger, twice the noise.

Defines love as anyone's surrender but his own.

Wolf's got a big smile— somebody's unhappy.

His fear imposes the faces within him on the faces without.

Never found kindness because he first sought the meanness behind it.

Cherry blossoms blow across the courtyard; he too once had smiles in excess.

The choices were between his life and his art, that seemed obvious. But should his art feed the life or his life feed the art? Which was the jewel and which the setting? Clearly his life would end, no doubting that; and while the art, or the praise it received, would also end, it might not end as quickly. Yet he would never know—whether his art lasted a week beyond his death or a thousand years, he would have no idea. So why not use his art as his life's tool? It could gain him a job, win him respect of a sort. He could hold up his head. It would be a career, a profession, and only the smallest interior voice would remain to accuse him of throwing away his dreams—a voice from his youth, an impractical voice.

The wrongs he had done came and went, were quickly over. Years later their echo rang in his ears undiminished.

When I see myself as without fault, I see myself as inhuman.

In his eagerness for joy, he pushed others into darkness.

She is angry he looks at her breasts; he is angry she gives him no place else to look.

A box of cobwebs, the self he protected for so long.

The betrayed friend: wasn't it his fault?

Like a child astride a merry-go-round lion, so he rode his anger.

Often to his chagrin he realized that the smiles of the previous evening expressed not pleasure but forbearance.

He knew it was foolish. He didn't flatter it by calling it ambition. But he dreamt of a labor that would keep him in the day: owning a shop, for instance, selling a few rare editions and old prints. His needs would be simple. He'd live upstairs, have a cat and never think of tomorrow till it crept through his bedroom window. In the evening, after work, he would drink a small coffee at the corner café, then stroll through the streets, exchanging greetings with his neighbors. At times he would stand on the bridge to watch the river churn and tumble far beneath. Leaning forward with his elbows on the parapet, he would look down at the mix of white froth and black water plunging between the stone arches. How awful to live like that, he would think, always moving, never at rest. And briefly he would try to imagine such a disorderly life before making his way home through the darkening city.

The moments he remembers—they would fill a single day.

After they gave him the prize, he dedicated his life to building his statue.

Cheapens his talent by wanting to be loved.

Being patient means putting aside fear.

Two crows on the branch of a dead oak: so his resentment waits.

Gardener thinks he digs better holes than the dog.

Young, he thought the answers lay ahead; older now, he thinks they must lie behind.

Yellow light through the pine trees—the road bends and climbs but still no end in sight.

You take a train through a foreign country. Noticing a farmhouse with a red tile roof set off among wheat fields, you imagine having been born there, a life tilling those fields. Or passing through towns with gray stone houses, you think, I could have lived there, I could have walked those streets. Even a chateau at the edge of a forest—what would that life have been like? Idly you wonder how you might return to those places, but you have no map, no idea of their names. Then in a station you see a woman on another train— she going south, you north. You look at each other with mild curiosity—an attractive woman, your age, perhaps a little younger. Soon your train pulls away, but now when you look at the countryside, those towns with pretty stone houses, you impose the woman's face across them. What a life you invent for yourself, what a small regret to burden your contentment. These attempted escapes from your accustomed routine that take you by surprise— you can almost hear the door again bang shut, the key grate in the lock.

Attentive only to his path, he didn't see those who had fallen until he joined them.

You are the song you are learning to sing.

Both jailer and prisoner see the world through steel bars.

He appears to be guarding a secret. His secret is that he has no secret.

Between his heart
and mind, he wore a
path unable to find
his rest in either.

When he praises you,
cover your wallet.

Rat grows fat on
foolish hopes.

Two seconds before
orgasm, he thinks of
the cosmos
ascending; two
seconds after, he
thinks of his bills.

His definition of beauty included light, his definition of peace included silence. Courage required physical resolution. Joy needed touch and color. Release called for the door to be flung open. Hope required the imaginary scaffolding of tomorrow's fulfillment. Faith was needed for conviction. An embrace meant corporeality. Rhythm meant force, the pounding of his heart. And certainly for passion he needed flesh and blood, warmth and palpability. But every one he found in music, which is invisible and drifts off on the least current of air.

Chose lead; paints it yellow.

Smart chicken—the one they roast on Sunday.

How he perceived the world became the barrier between himself and the world.

When people avoid his company, he blames it on the sparks cast off by his genius.

Joyless himself, he saw another's joy as weakness.

Even his tombstone was crooked.

Three balls: one for talking back.

Wishes he could take his lesson from the river, feels most persuaded by the stone.

Sometimes confusion was a veil across his eyes. Then what he loved became suspect, what he had disliked he now despised. Colors grew darker, sounds sharper. In his blindness, he trusted nothing and he struck out at whomever came too close. Better to be alone than betrayed; better to have no one trespass on the space he saw as his. So he hid and gnawed himself and was unhappy. But these times didn't last long—perhaps a week, no more. When he was returned to the world, he expected his friends and family to celebrate his recovery, now that his love had been restored. Surely, they would welcome his homecoming. Instead, they kept their distance, seeing him at last in clarity as lately he had seen them in confusion.

Between his eyes and the object of his sight, his yesterdays
writhed and tumbled.

When he felt death growing within him, he named everything
except what it was. Death waited. It was more patient than the
others. This is what made it death.

He used his solitude not to increase his life but to worry about
what was missing.

Right now, in other rooms, your children glance around in
wonder.

In time he replaced his fantasies about the future with dreams of
how he might have chosen differently in the past.

You call him smart when he says what you would have said had
you thought of it first.

Long after his friends had died, he saw their features in the faces
of others. This helped him to love others.

His first problem was to learn how to live. When he grew
distracted by a lesser problem—fear, jealousy, resentment—then
he forgot how to live.

He loved his joy as a road out of himself just as a building needs a door, otherwise it becomes a prison. And at times it seemed a prison was all he had—defeats, mistakes, the endless repetition of minutiae, while ahead stretched a succession of obligations like stones out of which his walls were built. And what dismal walls they made: the concrete mildewed and cracked, no windows or place to sit. But then, with his hope all but overthrown, morning sunlight would send a bright wedge across the floor, his wife would touch his cheek, the piano's notes would rise toward their crescendo. At once the door would fly open and he would be gone, rushing again through the capricious world.

The joy he took in each day unsettled the skeptics' unclouded vision.

Clean on the outside because he can't get at the inside.

If I see change as loss, it becomes loss.

Rich, handsome—it wasn't his attention that women distrusted, but his wish to see if they deserved his attention.

Listen: your ego isn't on your side. It has its own side.

His fear of ridicule kept him from singing.

What is terrifying is not the unknown but how I will enter it.

Pocket full of keys, owns nothing.

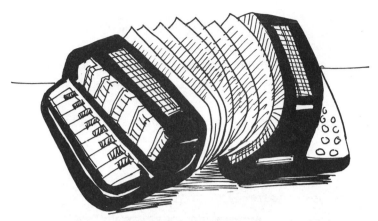

A love of music, nearly perfect pitch—without knowing it he had a gift to play the accordion. He even loved that sort of music—polkas and tangos, beer hall music—and had he begun to play, he might have been among the best. But the idea never occurred to him and no one suggested it. Not that he was a failure. He had a good job, an adoring family, but his successes were not like those he might have had if he had played the accordion. Mediocre lawyers with the exact hands of surgeons, painters who should have been poets—how often does a person take a wrong turn or doesn't find the right one? A decent life lived by default while the triumphant goes begging. One day a man looked in a shop window and saw the accordion: black enamel, ivory keys, mother-of-pearl buttons. His breath quickened and he nearly went inside, but he had someplace important to get to, so he turned up his collar and hurried away.

As a man crossing a desert tosses aside his backpack and empty canteen; so, as he grew older, he cast off dream and ambition.

His righteousness increased as his faith in his abilities decreased.

Talks like a dictionary; farts like a mule.

When he admires the rose, he admires all that he is not.

Hold the stone in the palm of your hand. Try to think of yourself like that.

Rabbit trusts only its fear.

Mouse grows proud, invites the cat to tea.

The cute laugh that first drew him to her became in time a splinter in his brain.

He knew his vulnerabilities and concealed them: Nostalgia, naïveté, wonder. They could hurt him in the long run—inviting ridicule as sugar attracts flies. So every sunset, well, he'd seen better. Luxury, women, the routine frontiers of pleasure—he gave the impression that something was always missing. But deep inside he was the child singing alone in an empty room—chipped white paint and bare floors, late-afternoon light through a single window. Still, the concessions of adulthood had strained his voice, his song was smaller—nothing like the symphonies he had composed when young, his astonishment's rich polyphony. And yet this present song—this melodic whicker, a groan of several notes, a droning bombination—what else remained to help him begin the day and accept those compromises which the day would force upon him in return?

This one was kind because he had not yet been hurt. That one was kind because he had been hurt often.

Puts a sock in his shorts to look virile, a book on the shelf to look smart.

Let humility be a weapon.

Eats sugar; tastes salt.

He keeps a moth in his wallet to remember the past.

One day he shows off his muscles, the next he shows off his cane.

To enter old age gracefully requires the forgiveness of the child he once was.

You have been sent as messenger, but you know neither the message nor whom it is for.

At the ocean he studied the waves—how they built and broke, their regularity and variety. It seemed meaningful, yet no meaning came to him beyond a sense of boundless space. But ships crossing the horizon, the shapes of clouds, the calligraphic patterns sketched by flocks of birds—even these articulated part of his question, an enigma almost understood. Then he would wait, holding his breath, as the tension grew and at last dissolved into nothing. Yet when he walked back to his car it seemed that an answer had indeed been given, but an answer beneath the level of thought, which his body grasped as his mind thrashed and faltered. So he kept coming back, watchful and uncertain, to observe the waves enact their repetitions, thinking that part of the mystery had been revealed, even feeling better for it, yet unable to break through the mist—he refused to call it confusion—that filled the spaces between knowledge and unknowing.

Horse's hooves on paving stones. The man lifts his head from his book, momentarily freed from dishonesty and dreaming.

All the words I use to distinguish me from others make me resemble others.

It is not his needs that he finds frightening; rather, he is afraid of not needing.

Only when he grew jealous did he decide he must be in love.

Prick claims to lift up the whole world with one foot.

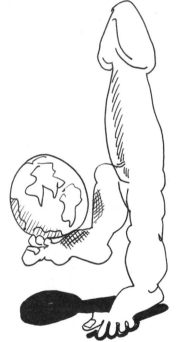

Seek to disarrange. It's the ultimate arrangement.

Love exists not in what is embraced, but in what is released.

The sense of awe that once expanded his life with possibility now filled him with foreboding.

In some dreams he could run: great effortless strides, as if his body were weightless or gravity defeated. But in the waking world, his running days were over. Bad knees had reduced his attempts at haste to a clumsy stumble. Even when he had run five miles a day it hadn't been like this—the elation and effortless vaulting ahead, not running from anything or toward anything, rising twenty feet, then descending as lightly as a leaf. The joy of such times lingered long after waking and he didn't know whether the dream was meant to mock him or to comfort him, because how heavy his tread had become in the realm of his vigilance, how slow were his footsteps as he approached one after another of the world's doors: at times gaining entry, at times being turned away.

Those things he sought—whenever he found them quickly he thought himself lucky, not that he had been mistaken in what he sought.

Art dictates; decoration distracts.

Wolf thinks the sheep wants to be eaten.

A million sonnets composed on the toilet.

Mouse builds up its muscles; cat lounges about.

Justified his faults by pointing to his many virtues.

Afraid that it would weaken his judgment, he denied beauty a place in his life.

Soon he will resume his burden. In morning sunlight, the sparrow hops across old snow.

The pleasure of creating something—it was like theft. Nothing had to be given back. A poem, a picture, a song—patched together from inner scraps: a few words on paper, a perception, the memory of a warm wind across water, fading light on red brick, wind riffling the wheat. Ha, he'd think, I've gotten something for free. Yet as time passed he felt ever more constricted, his vitality diminished. Anger and tears drew closer together as he gave himself up with ever-smaller gestures. He realized he was shrinking into himself. Even his shadow seemed paler and the light shone through him as it might through a shred of worn cloth held up to the moon. How foolish to think no payment was due; his error was in not learning the price.

He is the shadow of what others imagine him to be. And how he sees himself, others see the shadow.

You will be defeated. There is no changing this. Fight harder.

Perhaps music settles him because it is all that he is not.

Every farewell is a greeting to the dark.

So rich was his life's feast that his tombstone split from the force of his postmortem farts.

Shoots his sperm into the air, waits for the rainbow.

Be generous with your scorn. Let it feed on you as well.

When he had two things to accomplish in a single day and only completed one—no matter how successfully—he felt he had wasted the day.

For one it was the wish to be loved, for another a wish to escape, for a third a wish for revenge, for another the wish to be of use, then the wish for connection, the wish to be amusing, the wish to be admired. Others can be imagined. Who knew their source? The dim corners of early life, some lack or early encouragement? But each desire took precedence over any other, each had its own motivating force, and each person conveyed his private longing to any gathering as a sort of special guest, the recipient of all conversation and behavior. The one who wished to be loved was always listening for that special nuance of kindness; the one who wanted revenge always kept himself ready, while the actual moment—wedding or funeral—hardly mattered as the man or woman waited for the declaration of something begun long before conscious remembering. Is this true of everyone? Someplace this vacancy exists, this sweet location, this ache—a mystery which even its victim can't recall but which decides each day's action and worries him to sleep at night.

The uniqueness of which he felt so proud: a web of desire surrounding a scrap of common sense.

It wasn't wisdom that made him seem dignified but his fear of seeming foolish.

Read books searching for the life he had hoped to live.

He claims to have lost everything yet still has breath to complain.

Only gives you a hug when others are watching.

Hurries home to greet the person who is never waiting.

Be grateful for suicide. Otherwise how claustrophobic you would feel.

Lays his head on the pillow; another day without being found out.

He prided himself on his honesty and refused to think that his faults were due to self-deception; rather, in the empty space between virtue and venality, he constructed another figure, a simulacrum of himself, which he fed and clothed and pushed into the world. It lived his life at those times when he turned away, averting his eyes and adopting a sort of highbrow negligence, which he liked to call naïveté. It defended his appetites, voicing the preferences of his voracity and taking the blame. It nibbled the cake he pushed aside. Did he mind that it blundered along and bore little resemblance to how he saw himself? It became the only self he had.

Your children's uncertainty when they look at you. Isn't this a condemnation?

His wish to destroy was preceded by his wish to be right.

Monkey jeers at the lion for not being a monkey.

Each distraction was a rope hanging from the window of his personal bedlam.

You drop your poems into the dark. Do you imagine the space will be filled?

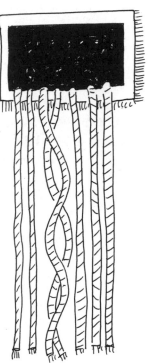

What he called clear-sightedness, those around him called distrust.

Once won a horse race, now he claims to tell the future.

You listen to them quarrel about the chimera of language; without words they are nothing.

The wish had been there all along—to open a door and step out of himself. As a child he had thought it possible to escape to a cloud (he could hop from a hilltop). Drugs, alcohol, sex: all had been doors. Beauty was a door. Laughter was a good door, he would have liked more of that. Love, food, the curve of a breast—doors of many sizes. Sorrow, ugliness, despair led no place. They only repeated the problem. Yet after sex, after the prizes, he was back again. He couldn't get out and stay out. Who knew why? It wasn't for want of trying. In his last years, he built his tomb: a philosophical assertion about the Great Beyond in the Great Before. Of course it had a door—brass hinges, brass doorknob, then a Judas hole to see who had come to visit, what the trees were doing and watch the clouds in their flight across the sky.

Mouth too small for the world; belly too big.

Makes a bad choice; points to his broken path.

Snail praises the tortoise for its speed.

What is most mysterious is not what is absent, but what surrounds you.

You are a yowl with a mouth attached and a body to carry that mouth.

Crawls on his belly, calls it tact.

The first task of his self-deception was to hide all signs of self-deception.

Not till the first shovelful of dirt hit his coffin did he ask how to live.

For years he thought madness must be peaceful—a positive letting go—and he looked forward to a time when he would no longer need to hold on like a man hanging from a high branch. He even thought it would be restful, as if madness were an interior spa where he could reclaim himself before rejoining the daily agitation. As a result, he hadn't expected the noise, the discord, like a radio stuck between stations, a multitude of voices, each with advice, entreaties, commands, but hardly audible, just noise, static, no way to bring it to a halt, and vexing him even as he slept. Now he knew that if he found his way back, he would work harder, be reliable. Such were his promises, but the choice was no longer his to make. It had become confused with the tumult, the racket, like a motor rushing out of control, pistons rattling, metal fracturing, gobs of oil flung off.

There is much you don't like. Which falls on the side of philosophy, which on laziness?

One bad yesterday and he grieves over a week of tomorrows.

Perhaps he is kind because he is not yet ready.

This one carries the question mark as a burden, that one as a gift he is glad to have been given.

Pockets full and still whining.

Another's pleasure increases his sense of loss.

The more he grew satisfied, the more restless became his dreams.

The sky darkens, waves trouble the lake's surface: you always have felt far from home.

It was the lack of certainty that disturbed him. First a thing was one way, then another. His mood, physical well-being, his emotions—in an instant all could change. Thing, thing—the very word mocked him with his want of knowledge. So he improved his speech, honed his meanings making them more exact, while with his syntax, the modulation of his voice, even a mounting fervor he was able to enshrine each ambiguity within a treasure house of discourse. Now, although he knew no more than before, his intensity and verbal glitter bore the likeness of knowledge, seeming to prove that his earlier doubts had been mistaken, and so for him and others his ignorance passed for wisdom, as if he had taken a mongrel from the street, taught it to walk on its hind legs, then to wear a coat and tie until soon it sat on his left at dinner, said please and thank you, and even passed the roast beef.

Once again autumn begins its slow advance. Leaf by leaf the seasons strip you of your place in time's mansion.

Tomorrow is given a thousand names which death retracts.

When we speak with one another, we confirm our isolation.

Truth, for a dog, is a full belly; for a man it's an empty one.

Stands on the flagpole to hide the holes in his shoes.

Do you wish to tell the truth or wish to be believed?

Hates to share his sunset with others.

A cat's not cruel; it's simply efficient. Only a creature that has felt compassion can be cruel.

To stand on a high place, a cliff over the ocean, seeing pelicans circle, at first ungainly, then plunging like flung stones—this was what he loved under a gray sky with a rough sea, no beach, a rocky coast and the distant sound of the surf, a rumble and crash and hissing away. He felt sure that when he died his specific light would flick out, no more than that, and at times he looked forward to its dark repose. But at other times he thought that if he had had a previous life, he must have been an albatross, one of the smaller ones, nothing regal. That would have given him joy, instead of today's to-ing and fro-ing, its altercations and constricting chambers. And no matter how much he believed in the coming dark, at times he wished the other might lie ahead—riding the air currents with nothing to hinder his vision of the horizon, that gray line between shifting cloud and unsettled water.

What he called his objectivity was a bit of smoke between his attention and his fear.

He loved in order to be increased, not in order to love.

When he praises others, they feel worse.

Dips his words in honey; you still taste the salt.

Peeks into the houses of his neighbors to measure their happiness against his own.

Spent his youth, still waits for the prize.

When an object is given value, it becomes debased.

You were born to be destroyed: find joy here.

He loved the general over the particular, the idea over the application. So when he gave of himself, he always kept something back, though not from a lack of generosity. Was it trust that was missing? First you give the hand, then they want the arm? Was he being cautious? Of course others saw his hesitation—the welcome extended, then withdrawn—and without his commitment, they held back as well. This ambivalence or indecisive gesture—where did it come from? He hardly knew it existed. But so it was between himself and the world: a series of checked invitations, a music that briefly engaged him, a dance of shadows as he and his partners circled each other, reaching out and almost touching, but not touching as he spun away to the silence of his life.

He grew so disfigured by his years of deception that he became foreign to himself—as much a mystery at the end of his life as at the beginning.

He never minded his faults until they blossomed in his children.

Between him and the blank page—all his doubts lived there.

Feels virtuous when he resists what he never wanted.

The woman he chose as the companion on life's journey, in time, as his love increased, became the journey itself.

Even a stone believes it can dance.

Dead rabbit: depended on the goodness of others.

Refused to take chances for fear of risking what he called his good name.

Birdsong, sunsets, the oak's black outline against the winter sky—how often natural beauty weakened his resolve. Moonlight on the lake's unsettled surface, butterflies among the daylilies—such displays diminished the world's marketplace, cooled his economic ardor. Beneath the shadow of nature's flashy here and now, salesmen with their horns and breathy guarantees became no more than lackluster hucksters of the ersatz and gaudy. Better to have tin birds and pine trees of papier-mâché. The sooner the earth received a coat of plaster and concrete, the sooner would fashion erase what simply was. Comfort, tranquillity, even pleasure—better to confine them to the future as goals to work for, stratagems to make him persevere.

Distrusted happiness because at such times he forgot who he was. This was also why he sought it.

Sat in a straight chair during the day so he could sleep in a feather bed at night.

The shame that his misconduct awoke in him: he called it modesty.

Spent each day grieving for the day before.

Tears his coat into ten pieces, calls it a wardrobe.

Nothingness frightened him only when he imagined himself something.

The edifice of one's work requires death to precede the driving of the final nail.

What do you hate? All that commodifies the world. What do you love? The useless, what finds no place in institutions. Don't call it beauty. Call it breath.

He felt best moving between two points—leaving New York, not yet entering Massachusetts; entering a store, not yet making a purchase. Even intellectually that was where he felt best—moving between two ideas, leaving one, not yet embracing another. And women—leaving one, not yet charming the next. He felt safest between guarantees, when he could take a thing without being anything himself, when transition itself seemed proof of success, even at times granting him the illusion of progress. Later, when a goal was reached and he needed to commit himself, then new difficulties arose, defects became obvious, at least until he began moving again—places, ideas, women, staying ahead of what came behind and a step short of arrival. Here all covenants were golden, dream became substance. Here, for a few moments, a day, a week, he never doubted his mastery.

He chose truth not from virtue, but from fear of losing himself in falsehood's back alleys and culs-de-sac.

Love doesn't need a reason; hate needs a reason.

He abused his power: he kept using it to see if it worked.

Ties a ribbon around his prick but can't teach it to say please.

Medusa's face in the shield of Perseus: how many mornings did he see his face like that?

Feels he should be repaid for his moments of kindness.

He loves you till you're out of sight.

Feeds meat to his laughter, lets his wonder eat cake.

His failures—could he blame them on time? He hadn't been ready when the lucky chance arrived. Or if not time, then perhaps the fault was how he reacted to time's upheavals—those surprises that seemed to come from nowhere. And often at the moment of success, the success was less than expected, smaller than deserved. So weren't his defeats the result of high expectations? He had worked hard, but the outcome wasn't what he hoped. Indeed, it was unfair. But who could say what was fair and what wasn't? Hubris, arrogance, self-love: wasn't it pride that said what he should have? What he had to have? Those setbacks—weren't they the result of an inner voice that said he deserved better, a voice that sang to him, soothed him and had never told the truth?

Resting his hand on the hand of another—the moment when his sense of separation felt greatest.

Would rather smile than think.

Brags about buying ten condoms for a penny.

Decks out his ignorance with diamonds and pearls—calls it knowledge.

Boat adrift on the pond: where shall he travel from here?

Flies fifty flags, gives allegiance to none.

For the cat no remorse; for the mouse no retribution.

Little by little, what he learned about himself led him to let go of what he thought he had learned about the world.

Friends with whom he had quarreled, friends who had moved away, friends who had died—how their numbers grew. The people he had loved and loved still and who had left his life, they would fill a small village—one he might drive through late at night in early fall—a dozen lights burning and only the Laundromat open. Perhaps the wind has changed and through the car window comes the smell of turned earth and burning leaves—surely he could live in a town like this, find contentment, and for a moment he feels the touch of its cracked sidewalks beneath his feet, knows the owner of a barking dog and who is awake in an upstairs window where a light still burns. Then it is gone; the fields are dark and the road stretches ahead, indifferent and unexplored.

When a friend dies, he stays at your elbow—bumping it, bumping it, until you yourself push him into shadow.

The loneliness of living made him terrified of the loneliness of death.

His hope sets plastic roses in the desert of his future.

Naps in a cemetery to stop worrying about time.

Hangs a padlock on his zipper; calls himself good.

When he is silent, he imagines he is being brave.

Scratches his balls when he thinks; scratches his head when he pees.

Beauty on one side, ugliness on the other: the difference was his wish to find a difference.

So skillful grew his rhetoric of seduction that those he charmed be-
came no more than the nodders and scrapers of his oratory. Even
his skeptics vanished, since his words discredited them with those
who believed. But to him his believers became faceless. They were
changed into other: the apparatus he used for his stratagems. He
grew to despise them even as he said how much he loved them. At
first he had flattered in order to increase himself, then to increase
the size of his domain, but the more he was trusted, the more the
world shrank and the more he had to expand the enormity of his
lie. How troublesome it was. What good was celebrity when his
dominion turned barren and his followers appeared stunted, no
more than particles of sand in a Sahara of his making?

It wasn't desire that impelled his many seductions, but the need to prove himself desirable.

Blue sky, green grass: the cow has no fear of tomorrow.

Cat watches the mouse hole; rat steals the kittens.

Pimple boasts of being a boil.

Eats as if searching for the thing he has lost.

The less he has to say, the louder he says it.

Alone, he imagines himself captain.

Your enemies have defined the world without you.

At times he tried to locate the moment of change—a question that might occupy him if he were driving a long distance or if his plane were delayed and he had to wait in an airport. He would think of the period in his childhood when he had believed the world benign, when he would speak to each person on the street and that person would speak back with a sort of surprised smile. Then his shyness had begun. The long progression of days of grace, his reprieve from knowledge, had grown uncertain. You never knew what might happen next. You never knew how a person might react—anger or benevolence. He could guess the year of the change, but recalled nothing that seemed significant: no trauma or sudden awareness. Was it no more than an amassing of negative detail, a sudden tilt toward understanding? Yet who was he to call it negative? Might it be only the nature of wisdom? Yet what made it wisdom? Perhaps it was just the world's customary unfolding. Then he would reach the town to which he had been driving or his plane would be called. He would shrug off his thoughts, walk to the gate. By the time he was settled in his seat, his question would be forgotten.

Increasingly as he sat with a friend who was dying, he saw not the friend's face, but his own.

The more he loved the world, the less he saw the abyss; the more he stared at the abyss, the less he loved the world.

He was born with a ring of silver that grew darker and tarnished with age, but it was still a ring of silver.

Evening light against a row of shops—why does his sense of beauty contain a sense of farewell?

When he claims to tell the truth, he reveals his entire sense of value, whether he lies or tells the truth.

Resembles a dog on the brink of an idea.

Those men who desired her—she felt she stood on their shoulders.

As he aged, dream and memory grew so entwined that recollection became his most fertile source of fantasy.

His want formed a craving never satisfied. The things he bought, food he ate, the women he desired—it was a fire he couldn't snuff out. I need this, he would say, and his longing grew so huge that if it were fulfilled, it seemed he would never need again. Yet his joy in acquisition lasted rarely a day, then his need shifted to something else, some person or object or adventure he had to have. But nothing brought relief and he saw that if he could have all he longed for, then it would still be like having nothing, that the need existed separately from satisfaction, as if only death could stop his hunger, as if what he actually craved was death itself in a variety of shining disguises that time itself would strip away, leaving at last the final thing, the ultimate commodity, which would overspread him and draw him within, then shut the light.

The soul is a tourist; the body seeks a home.

The gravedigger never weeps.

Hears a siren, looks for a parade.

Still sniffs his fingers after he wipes.

She chose beauty over language. Now she is ugly and full of complaint.

Stomach growls; mouth trembles.

In time he learned to limit his expectations to expectation itself.

When he tries to explain the beauty of the rose, he begins by describing the earth around it.

Over a cup of coffee or sitting on a park bench or walking the dog, he would recall some incident from his youth—nothing significant—climbing a tree in his backyard, waiting in left field for a batter's swing, sitting in a parked car with a girl whose face he no longer remembered, his hand on her breast and his body electric; memories to look at with curiosity, the harmless behavior of a stranger, with nothing to regret or elicit particular joy. And although he had no sense of being on a journey, such memories made him realize how far he had traveled, which, in turn, made him ask how he would look back on the person he was now, this person who seemed so substantial. These images, it was like looking at a book of old photographs, recognizing a forehead, the narrow chin, and perhaps recalling the story of an older second cousin, how he had left long ago to try his luck in Argentina or Australia. And he saw that he was becoming like such a person, that the day might arrive when he would look back on his present self as on a distant relative who had drifted off into uncharted lands.

Nothing totally exists which is coming into being and when it totally exists it is over.

Puppet lands on the trash heap ignorant of its strings.

When he worries, he imagines he thinks.

Tries to salt your broth as well.

Smiles to hide his teeth.

Says please; means now.

Goes to the whorehouse to sprinkle his dreams with glitter.

Those things he saw in terms of their usefulness, he had yet to see them.

How he nurtured his cynicism. He'd been in love. He'd been ambitious. Projects and journeys had been begun. There had even been successes. But between his ego and his disappointments, cynicism rested on its cushion: "Life was like that." "Their treachery was clear from the start." "It was bound to happen." In this way, total failure was avoided and strength was found to start again. Most of this strength went to new schemes, which surely would succeed, but the choicest scraps fed his cynicism to keep it ready against future defeat. So he never gave himself completely to any new effort; his cynicism had to be kept safe. Couldn't this be a cause of failure? On the contrary, he saw himself as like a general who holds troops in reserve to protect the army in retreat, rejoicing after each loss about what had been saved; while that reserve guard, the very sum of his cynicism, always it was the first to applaud his cunning.

Before he could be cruel, he had to imagine himself important.

He calculates the cost of future sins in terms of past apologies.

Most in danger when you feel safe.

All his gifts were the gift of dead flowers.

With his club he guarded two paths: outward to the world, inward to the imprisoned self.

Does it itch? Live longer, don't scratch it.

Everything that breathes will be eaten.

His moments of solitude were the paving stones on the road to his vanishing.

Such days as these—radiant afternoons in late fall, the weather so mild that you can sit in the backyard and let the sun caress your face. No leaves, of course. An early frost has finished the flowers though some marigolds are left along the path. Just last week there were snow flurries, and storms are stranding travelers in the west. These gifts that arrive in late season—a sudden rush of happiness, bursts of creative work, even an unforeseen love affair. Already winter has laid its finger upon your cheek and now comes this reprieve. It would be foolish to think it more than brief. It would be foolish to make plans. You have just this afternoon—the thing itself. You rest your head against the back of your chair and shut your eyes. Behind your closed lids the light turns pink. Then some noise distracts you and you lift your head. The pines extend their shadows across the lawn. How soon the sun begins to set.

Timid, he saw the successes of others as proof of their presumption.

To watch the sunset: isn't it to see an argument formulated?

When he is cruel, he imagines he was driven to it.

Chose the solitary path, brags of it to others.

Only in the dark does he dance a silly dance.

Foreman shows up, hammers make a racket.

He thinks his erect prick articulates the winning side of an argument.

He could speak of nothing but things and so he came to call them ideas.

When he felt most loved, he felt most burdened. He didn't know why. Did he feel unworthy or pressed too close? Perhaps he felt that if he came to depend on this love, then he might be injured if it gave way. Perhaps he felt too big a thing would be asked of him, too big an obligation. At such times he began to think of isolation, the quiet of the forest in winter, the depth of a cave where he could sit with his back to a rock, listening to the erratic drip of water. And after a while, he would go there, if only in his mind. He would remain in the cave's damp twilight, neither happy nor sad, till someone came who cared enough to lead him back to the world, to draw him into the sunlight. But as time passed, fewer people were left to bring him back and at last none at all. Then he forgot that he had ever been outside or had loved, had been loved, or had ever known more than the rock walls and shadow.

Those things he failed to understand, didn't they exist just to make him look foolish?

He keeps eating in order not to share.

When I am feared, I am weakened.

Whitewashes the past; colors the future.

Farts in public: points to the pig.

The fatter his wallet, the louder his complaint.

Tomorrow rubs its hands, yesterday wrings them.

What he called his sorrow was simply a full life minus what his vanity had told him he deserved.

He felt bullied by his possessions. One needed fixing, another to be returned to its shelf. One needed reassembling, another taken apart. Each had demands that must be met to keep it working. These gadgets meant to enrich his life—in their mass they came to control him so that instead of being added to, he felt decreased. In bed at night, he could hear them whisper: Repair me, make use of me, plug me in—until he felt their loathing as he passed through his rooms. They had expected a superior home and he failed to win their respect. In time he began to spend longer and longer periods in the backyard, avoiding his house altogether, which seemed to shudder and jerk like a bag full of cats. These things he owned, wasn't he now the possession of his possessions, their knickknack or novelty, as if he had been changed into one of those door prizes handed out at awful parties, a grimacing, plaster statuette, displayed on the mantel for a few weeks before being banished to the attic?

He defines himself not by looking at what he is but by looking at the choices he didn't make.

When in a crowd, he feels alone; when alone, his mind swarms with faces.

He grew ignorant when he stopped asking questions to give answers.

Disapproves of another's actions to show the value of his own.

Tiger keeps a bit of fear to sharpen its claws.

Defeated in the race, he runs another mile to show it isn't over.

Every parting is a missed opportunity.

Be kind. Watch carefully. Bear witness to what you see. What else is required of you?

In the beginning, he was like a crowd leaving a circus—memory of noble lion tamers, clowns, trapeze artists spinning at the top of the tent. Then one person split off from the rest, then another. These were the choices he could have made but didn't, the ones he set aside—that move to California, the woman he chose not to marry, the job it seemed too risky to take. As time passed, more people split away and his choices diminished. Then it was no longer like a crowd leaving a circus. Few options remained; the end began to emerge. Do you recall those dances when you were young and the boys or girls would hurry across the floor to pick their partners? Sometimes you would be left till last and across the floor would be one other—the partner no one wanted: hulking and graceless. That's the one you see now, your final partner, no choice about it.

What you call the world are twinkling lights between you and the mystery.

When he lied or cheated someone, he took pride in his faults as if they were virtues.

You don't offend me when you offend me. I offend myself.

Down the river of his life he paddled his canoe of complaint.

His immortality lasted until they threw out the flowers.

No dream, no disappointment; no imagination, no courage.

As he grew older, the women who returned his glance appeared on the street later and later.

Dead leaves drift across the roadway: he thinks of all he has lost.

Of course he saw that his dislike of received ideas and his quest for originality issued from the same source, but the subject baffled him. Couldn't the wish for originality itself be a received idea? As for newness, perhaps what he saw as new was no more than eccentric or odd, like putting ketchup on a banana. But how could he say what was not and what had never been? Who could tell him if he was on the right track? What did it mean to be original? He might spend years wasting his time. Instead, he decided to take the established form—the received idea—and rework it just a little. He would make it charming, clever, even make it vague so it couldn't be seen clearly or measured exactly. People would be forced to judge its appearance, rather than the thing itself. And that blend of mystification and obscurity, couldn't he claim that it was innovation?

In the morning he added up his strengths; in the evening he subtracted his failings.

Calls his good luck destiny, his bad luck conspiracy.

To the fly, it's all sugar.

Likes to count up the money he would have made had he chosen not to be good.

Only when the phone rings past midnight does he remember what he owes the world.

Minute barely started and he's two miles through the next.

Love is unqualified. His dislikes live in his qualifications.

What he called his understanding meant feeling comfortable with his ignorance.

Such pleasures he had taken in books—not the popular best-sellers, those ephemera of current fashion, but the great literature of the past: Greek tragedy, Elizabethan drama, the Russians. And Beethoven quartets, the operas of Richard Strauss, Caravaggio's paintings and Léger, to wander aimlessly through the great museums. But to look at his library over time was to see the popular fiction emerge—intelligent spy novels, the winners of the yearly prizes, then crime novels alone, though brilliantly plotted and wonderfully distracting. As for museums, he had already visited them. As for music, it made him moody and distracted, and more and more often his rooms were silent. In such a way did past and future vanish from his theorizing and he came to live only in the present, or such was his hope, with none of his yesterdays to measure himself against and nothing of the future to encourage his restless speculation.

When his options were no longer those associated with youth, he pursued those associated with money. They filled him with a sense of vitality. They made him feel youthful.

Wins a contest, feels underpaid.

Disillusionment and morality fatten side by side.

Waltz king in the houses of his friends, at home he trips over the dog.

She felt the only purpose of another woman's beauty was to diminish her own.

Temptation beckons; desire binds.

Those who believed his flattery, could he ever trust them?

This one takes his lesson from the thorn; that one from the flower.

When he was making love and slipped himself into the body of another, he was surprised at how the world vanished, was simply forgotten. His habit of rationalizing and theorizing, all he had built and had built upon—everything was in that instant trivialized. It amazed him that he had chosen to spend his life in any other way. Surely he would live each moment differently after this. What was his orgasm but fervent clarity? And later? Once again he resembled one of those dogs seen at twilight, loping along with its tail slack, its tongue slung loose, darting glances into passing faces, toward houses where the lights were coming on, but finding none to claim him, none of his own.

Defines the world to make it smaller.

Tries making his bed while still tucked within warm sheets.

When he begs your forgiveness, he believes he is doing you a favor.

With your crow call you summon the crows. They are confused and can't make out the message. Do you want your art to be like this?

At the moment of inspiration, he thinks he hears posterity's breathing quicken.

As his wisdom increased, so did his sense of fragility.

Without the poor, how would he feel wealthy? Without the ignorant, how would he dare speak?

Like touching a sore place, once he has seen the abyss he is forever at its rim.

Harsh words, dismissive gestures, even a blow: to justify his anger he pointed to the world's unfairness and cruelty— faults that the world has in abundance. Do you see, he might say. How could I feel otherwise? But he would say this even if the world were perfect. His excuses were pretext, the doors he used to free anger from its cage. The newspaper, nightly news, even gossip on the street— all gave evidence of possible encroachment. Strangers in automobiles, people who pressed too close—all could set loose this anger within him, a watchdog patrolling the perimeter of what he felt he deserved, zealous guardian of his ego and pride. And who, or so he kept asking, wouldn't be angry in such a situation? By which he meant life itself.

The first time someone died who he loved, his grief was so great that it included within it grief for everyone who would die afterward.

He grew shy from fear of loving too much.

When he believed he felt nothing, he in fact felt everything.

He walked beside his false self as a child walks beside an older brother.

The family had a distinctive nose that passed through several generations. Now they are known for nothing but the nose.

Because his dog was forgiving, he felt cheapened by his acts of forgiveness.

Snappy rejoinders and his guests asleep in their beds.

No wish to pick each flower in the garden; no wish to fuck every woman under his regard.

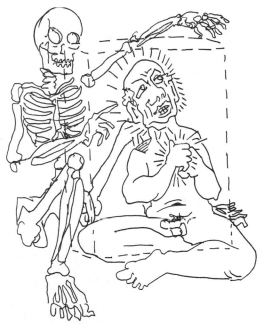

Friends of his youth, friends of his prime: they had been the audience for the stories of his ambition. But as he grew older, his listeners became fewer and his triumphs never materialized. Then, when he spoke with the more fortunate, it was to describe what had stood in his path, why he had never joined them—he had put his family first, he had offended certain critics. Without these obstacles, surely, there would have been no limit to his success. But even these listeners fell away; a new generation was hurrying down a road not his own, and behind that still another was preparing itself and no one knew or had any interest in his gifts. Soon he realized that he was receding into his own shadow. Indeed, in his final isolation the many versions of his story made up his tombstone: not one of marble but of living vapor, which his death—his ultimate listener—would, with a sympathetic whistle, casually disperse.

The pine's long shadow in morning sunlight: like this does his envy precede his applause.

When I give nothing away, I can call nothing mine.

A toy meant to dazzle—so he saw his learning.

In each of his choices, he tried to protect his past from regret.

Sweet to its mate: the porcupine's kisses.

He felt most secure believing in nothing—protected by something no one else wanted.

During the first half of his life, he looked up. During the second, he looked down. He never noticed the moment of change, nor even the difference.

A car passes on a rainy street. Waking, a man yearns for all that has vanished from his life.

When the leaves fell and the October wind shook the trees, he never thought that in five or six months the weather would turn warm and crocuses emerge from the soil. He could never see past winter itself, as if the season might get stuck, the wind keep blowing and snow heap up past the windows. And he was surprised it hadn't happened before, as if spring's yearly arrival was no more than good fortune. But this winter would be the long one. He felt sure of it. For a while he would dress warmly and tend the fire. He'd try to accustom himself to short days, the constant chill in his bones. Yet how long before his resolve gave out? Wasn't that what frightened him each fall—how long before he strayed from his path and walked out into the whiteness? Because in the whistling of the draft beneath the door, it seemed he heard a beckoning; in the wind through the trees he felt certain he heard his name being called.

His courage didn't lie in facing the day but in facing the darkness waiting behind it.

Smoke blowing across the rooftops: after she left what could bind him together?

More prayers than the pope, but don't lend him money.

He would have been satisfied with very little if everyone else had much less.

A tissue of learning, tissue of courtesy—the masks he put over the beast.

He liked a little vagueness, not knowing all the facts. The more he knew, the more he saw his mistakes.

By seeking to make art his ladder, he made it into a well.

That he was weak became his strongest defense.

At times it was in French or pages were missing or so covered with pictures that the words were hidden; once he had forgotten his glasses, twice he had to translate the words into his poor Spanish. As for the audience, once they had been sitting on the far side of a river, once at the rear of a huge hall, or they had their backs to him, told jokes to one another or knew only Greek. Other times he was across town and had one minute to reach the auditorium, or the elevator was broken, the train wouldn't come, he'd lost his keys. These public occasions when he read his work—what had he done for his sleeping self to exact such vengeance, as if he were bound to fail or the attention were undeserved? Dreams so arduous that he needed to rest after waking, then went to bed in a flinch. And all day they stayed with him as the lens through which he saw his life—his work pointless, the goal beyond his grasp— while he cursed himself and whipped himself after his ever-plunging ambition.

Old hopes and ambitions—he met them once again in the corridors of his nostalgia: secure, enduring and with their luster undiminished.

Parades his malice with morality's bass drum.

When he couldn't brag about his accomplishments, he bragged about his sufferings.

Doing wrong is not as bad as forgetting you have done wrong.

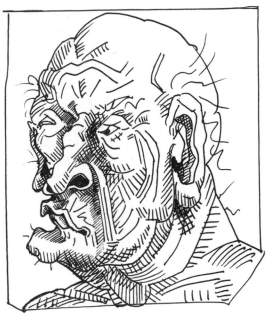

Once his teeth have been pulled, then he forgives.

His wife's tits are bigger than your wife's tits.

He didn't lose himself when he forgot himself, he grew larger.

Those things called real and lasting—the smallest breeze bears them away. Art attempts to fix them to one spot.

Say that each word is a board—sticks, solid timbers, sheets of plywood. Then outside and all around extends the darkness. What an elaborate scaffolding language has made, what an elegant complication of passageways and bulwarks, plankings and arches and ceilings. And look at what has been attached to the walls—philosophy, art, science, even fashion to show how such a place has always existed. Yet at times there is a sense of limitation; the corridors only extend so far. And at times a crack occurs—perhaps a question or sudden disturbance, perhaps decay or dissolution—then a shaft of darkness so dark that is like a shaft of radiance will break across the routine complacency. Or at times when one walks—who knows, perhaps there is a thin place where the night presses close, a certain insufficiency of definition—then at such times one will feel a trembling so slight that it might even be imagined. Breathe lightly, don't you feel it now?

Late September twilight, his footprints wind through the dust—
soon the first rains would erase them.

Gave a dime to a beggar, took it back when he wasn't thanked.

When I first learned language, I also learned suspicion and
distrust.

In his pocket he carried a clown's rubber nose as reason to love
the world.

Like wrestlers, his mind and
body constantly struggled.
The reason? See how the
darkness approaches and he
fails to notice.

The pleasures he had failed
to have diminished the ones
he had had.

Weasel needs only weasel
friends.

Let his principles take the
place of thought.

The more he considered his death, the more he felt certain it must be a handsome fellow—muscular, sharp-featured—perhaps a younger version of himself, somebody who had managed to avoid the moral and physical pitfalls which had caused his own road's mortal constriction. So, as he aged, his death became younger, healthier. Its loveliness increased. It regained the virtues of innocence, compassion, generosity: virtues that, if he had ever possessed, had diminished as his own troubles multiplied. Until at last, when his time came, his death had been transformed to pure possibility. It had all the future that he now had to do without. Eager and full of promise, it was the child who hurried forward to take him by the hand.

What frightened him was that there might be no mystery—only cash registers, politicians and the horizon.

When we touch others in kindness, the first person we touch is ourselves.

His fear made him trade his sense of wonder for a sense of consequence.

Those who failed to see the person behind her beauty were like travelers waylaid by thieves before reaching the safety of the next village.

Only the applause for the other person deafens.

Gets a free bowl of soup, demands a cloth napkin.

Your words stand next to their subject like pebbles beside a mountain.

When he wanted to learn about the light, he went to one who had studied the darkness, not to one who knew only the light.

His life was the practice of forming a single sentence which, as he grew older, he tried to simplify, reduce its compound-complex structure into one statement ruled by the single, inviolate pronoun within which he attempted to live, always engaged in revision and the act of becoming; as the distilled statement gradually became a fleeting inquiry, a mild interrogative that he repeated and refined, making it increasingly concise, almost, at his conclusion, producing no more than a single sound, not quite a word, less than a cry, which his death erased leaving the question mark hanging in the air, like a broken halo, emblem of his birth, evolution and release: a full life.

In the beginning he loved symphonies, vast landscapes, Gothic cathedrals; toward the end he loved a few bars of the quartet, a vein of marble, the interior of the hibiscus.

This one listens to hear what he hasn't heard; that one to hear what he has.

When he wanted to feel loved, he bought something.

Confuses what he desires with what he is owed.

By seeing his future as a goat's skull on a dung heap, he was able to value life's vast incandescence.

No trace of the perfect world you saw as a child. Art is its shadow.

Your heroes: those who fling themselves uselessly against the dark.

Does it matter that this one points to music, or that one to painting, or this other to the small troubles of his life? You did not choose your path; you have no complaint.

That day he and the woman spent hours on horseback on wooden saddles with layers of blankets, scrambling up and down hillsides over trails he would hesitate to take on foot. The sun burning through his shirt and hat; bristly thickets and cactus, sand, rock and red dirt: the path a faint track among darting lizards and dust-colored toads. Rising above them, mountains climbed past saguaro and organ pipe cactus to fields of snow so peaceful that he kept riding only to reach them as the trail ascended toward the distant passes. Then among the peaks he saw a bird but so high that he realized it must be immense, riding the air currents with a slight stirring of wings, tilting and sliding, a dark hardly discernible color as it dipped and soared. How did they appear from that alien free-dom—a man and woman on horseback, creeping earthbound creatures, hauling themselves inch by inch toward ever vanishing horizons?

PART TWO

DEFINITIONS

Abject: until you turn your back.

Abstinence: the tang of No in the mouth.

Abstraction: matter's kingdom come.

Absurdity: reason's fire escape.

Abundance: hands full and a little left over.

Abuse: to offend vanity's self-appraisal.

Abyss: the dark from where you hear your name whispered.

Accessory: the object you add to yourself in order to be yourself.

Accommodate: conditional surrender.

Accomplice: the one who takes the blame.

One's accomplishments: the fretful whistle between the self and
the dark.

Achievement: how long
  will he hang ribbons
  on the monster?

Acquisitive: greed with
  a credit card.

Age: not what you
  were promised.

Aggressive: someone
  entering the space
  you are about to
  absent.

Ambition: ladder made
  from the backs of
  others.

Ambivalence: cowardice in the abstract.

Amok: drops a frog down his secretary's blouse.

Anatomy: garden of earthy delights.

Anchorite: carries his balls in a satchel.

Anecdote: after-dinner
   soporific.

Anger: the fist I raise against
   myself.

Anonymous: retired.

Anxiety: four A.M. wake-up call.

Apathy: nothing you want to
   kiss back.

Archetypes: history's recurrent
   clichés.

Art: vehicle and destination.

Articulate: says what you wish to hear.

Artifice: lipstick on a skull.

Artless: shows off his five-dollar Rolex.

Ascendancy: big club versus big club
    with a spike.

Ascetic: prefers his mouth empty.

Asocial: chaperoned by his
    misgivings.

Authentic: convincing deception.

Autobiography: the embellishments of auto-enthusiasts.

Autodidact: proud of his ignorance.

Auto-fellatio: a perk lost by listening to serpentine seductions.

Autogamous: lyric poet.

Autumnal: dotage with a face-lift.

Bargain: the attempt to procure what is yours by right.

Bawdy: slipped his leash.

Beauty: reason's saboteur.

Bed: when you can't dance.

Behaves: puts his belly second.

Being: ennui's scullion.

Betrayal: his friends knew what was best.

Birthright: termination.

Blame: to diminish any person, place or thing.

Blather: one sentence too many.

Bliss: the past forgotten, the future unimagined.

Boast: seeks to add an inch to his small height.

Books: spoor of the beast we pursue.

Boredom: a lack of diversion making one focus on what exists.

Bosom: carnality's sweet divan.

Boss: pseudo-pal.

Boudoir: field of dreams.

Boundary: money's reach.

Bountiful: to give unnecessarily.

Bourgeois: brags even about his shit.

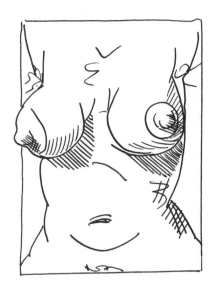

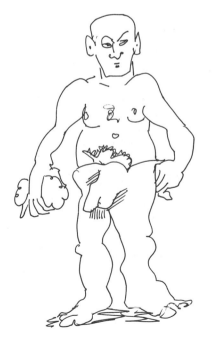

Bravado: two handkerchiefs stuffed into his underwear.

Bravery: to continue regardless.

Bray: the passionate articulation of secondhand convictions.

Breath: coinage. Be profligate.

Bric-a-brac: the cherished objects of another's aesthetic.

Bully: seeks outer validation of inner sophistry.

Bureaucrat: paper heart.

Cachepot: poet with a Ph.D.

Cadaver: post-promising.

Cajole: tickles your balls
with a feather.

Camouflage: smiles.

Candid: strategy for
introducing an untruth.

Capable: untalented.

Capitalist: gives his kisses to things.

Carapace: academic tenure.

Career: providential tumble down mortality's staircase.

Carnal: forages on
    others.

Cautious: wears two
    condoms at once.

Celibate: shoots his
    sperm inward.

Certainty: doubt's
    vestibule.

Chaos: the dominion
    beyond one's
    fingertips.

Charm: when you
    can't be good.

Chattel: little dumb friends.

Chauvinist: deaf to your side of the story.

Cinder: mortality's refuge.

Civic-minded: wants his own statue.

Civilize: to make someone over in your image.

Clever: scrap of praise reserved for dumb beasts.

Climax: the up preceding the down.

Clique: close-knit group of ex-friends.

Clothing: another of anxiety's disguises.

Coffin: farewell's dingy.

Committee: smarter than the pig; dumber than the butcher.

Complaint: animation's middle C.

Compliment: precedes a request.

Compost: inexorable denouement.

Conceited: melodious farts.

Concession: the crumb tossed to another's assertion.

Condolence: nevertheless, he must have deserved it.

Confident: suspension of disbelief.

Conformist: wishes to be thought worthy.

Confusion: liquefied opinions.

Conscience: inharmonious helpmate.

Constipated: no vices.

Consumer: equals ten rats.

Contempt: you have nothing he wants.

Contigent: another's truth.

Contradiction: truths from different
   times joined in one moment of time.

Conventional: the soul in white socks.

Convictions: rubber crutches.

Corpse: lately full of plans.

Correct: a monkey in a gang of monkeys.

Creation: a miscalculation in the
   backseat of the celestial limousine.

Credible: the tissue of equivocation
   momentarily intact.

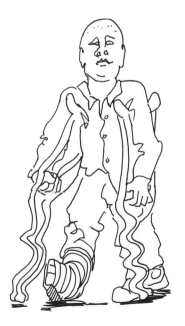

Crime: the publicity given his indiscretions.

Cultured: wears a ribbon on his hat.

Cynicism: when truth no longer helps.

Damage: the world exacts a fee.

Damned: wished to be safe; chose the second-rate.

Dance: the ever-flightless testing their wings.

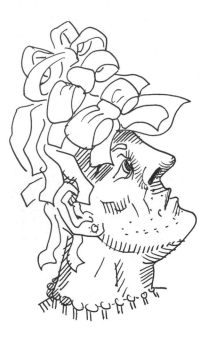

Dangerous: your boss suggests you shut the door.

Dawdle: endeavor's disavowal.

Daydreamer: ambition minus action.

Dazed: momentarily distracted from his mirror.

Death: a darkened lamp. Do you think the light went elsewhere?

Deception: the tongue's free agency.

Decrepitude: the tomorrow waiting in your shadow.

Definition: pup tent in
   bewilderment's snowstorm.

Demiurge: greenbacks at work.

Denial: morality's ground zero.

Dependable: still lends you money.

Depraved: wolves nibbling clover on
   the sly.

Depredation: the underhanded
   overturning of the undoubted by
   the unexpected.

Destiny: mortality's illusory carte du jour.

Diabolic: the wish to unsettle the seemingly fixed.

Dialogue: the eager agreement of your interlocutor.

Dictionary: brief hiatus in language's long flight.

Dignity: elevator shoes.

Digression: what the mouth does as the mind tries to think.

Discredit: easier than disputation, safer than violence.

Dissatisfied: one ear ever attuned to his inner chorale.

Doctor: ignorance in a white coat.

Dogma: a prettily carved stick to fend off the brute.

Duty: tends to others' business before his own.

Eager: belches before he eats.

Echo: better class of sycophant.

Eclectic: knows nothing well.

Eclipse: your shadow across his small light.

Economical: lets you pay the bill.

Education: varnished exhibition of society's apologia.

Ego: doorman of a building rising into the fog.

Elsewhere: where the good things happen.

Emancipation: the freeing of what you covet from the tyranny of others.

Emptiness: where you aren't.

Empty: the nose bag of all your expectations.

Encomium: when you can't give money.

Enigmatic: anything taking more than a moment's thought.

Ennui: the negative energy produced by a discharge of animating principle.

Enough: what others have.

Enthusiasm: three sticks for his drum and now he buys a bell.

Entice: deception's honeyed susurration.

Entropy: failure's scapegoat.

Épater le Bourgeois: tactlessly perseveres in describing what exists.

Epigram: a platitude in falsies, girdle and feather boa.

Erection: concupiscence's bantam oriflamme.

Erotic: an itch in the shorts unconnected to dirt, decay or insect life.

Erudition: necktie on a soapbox.

Esthetic: the rhetoric of bad taste.

Eternal: the moment after your last one.

Eulogize: the last chance to turn the blade.

Excrement: yesterday's escargot.

Excuses: resentment's bells and whistles.

Exemplary: hides his tracks.

Exhibitionist: two successes in a row.

Exile: prefers his own ideas.

Expediency: to push first.

Experienced: enough mistakes to get his attention.

Expert: detractors still in disarray.

Extraordinary: the shock of peering over the fence of too little imagination.

Fabrication: the gilded filigree of daily discourse.

Facility: as in "certain," referring to the genius of another.

Fait Accompli: the event before the excuses and whining.

Fame: a longer echo. There, it's gone.

Fantasies: unlimited options.

Fashion: the skeleton's gossamer boa.

Fear: premortem coffin.

Fervent: first with a bad idea.

Fib: mendacity's self-appraisal.

Finite: breaks before you break.

Flame: the recollected moments of one's life superimposed.

Flattery: someone's insincere disclosure of your personal truth.

Flatulence: corporeal wisecrack.

Flawed: triumph's obligatory carbuncle.

Flirtation: one toe in the water.

Flower: all we aren't.

Forbearance: what he calls his cowardice.

Forbidden: postponed pleasure.

Forgive: to delay retribution.

Fornicator: dances on one foot.

Fortitude: stubbornness in the face of evidence.

Fracas: your enemies at one another's throats.

Free: compensation deferred.

Free Will: the half step between forgetting and imagining.

Friend: the one who believes the lies you tell about yourself and whose lies you choose to believe.

Frugality: how he defines his selfishness.

Fulfilled: desire's impossible utopia.

Fun: self-forgetting.

Funeral: terminal pratfall.

The Future: whatever isn't.

Gadfly: complacency's implacable bad guy.

Gaiety: learned of his rivals' reversals.

Gallant: the fox offers the hen a petit four.

Garish: the wolf's wool sweater.

Gaudy: Day-Glo nipples in the
   whorehouse.

Gender: driving license.

Generosity: the soul's fingerprints.

Genteel: fartless.

Ghost: malingerer.

Gibe: heart dart.

Glamour: the body politic.

Glib: feather-tongued.

Gloat: basks in the sum of your ill fortune.

Glutton: uses his tongue as a blind
man uses his cane.

Goad: indignify.

Gossip: premature burial.

Graceless: lemon-footed.

Gratuitous: the vampire's thank-
you.

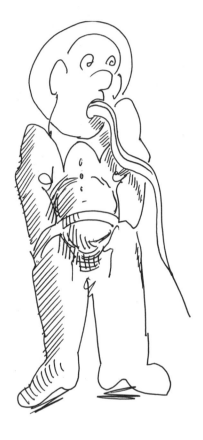

Grave: pockets empty at last.

Greed: two bellies, one for being
empty.

Gregarious: covert ambition's
rubber wheels.

Grievance: indignation's uplifted
finger.

Guarantee: the consecration of chattel.

Guest: your temporary better self.

Guile: appetite's padded feet.

Guilt: between the pleasure and forgetting.

Gullibility: the skeptic's prepubescence.

Habits: the mistakes he is best at.

Haggle: frugality's self-abasement.

Happy: learned to keep his eyes shut.

Harass: the unsolicited gift of your point of view.

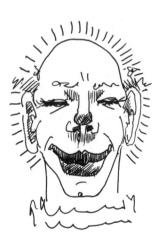

Harness: society's trade-off.

Harridan: former sexpot.

Harvest: decrepitude's gold watch.

Hate: the heart's clenched muscle.

Havoc: the hooded figure bursting from the birthday cake.

Heart: tomorrow's cinder.

Heartbreak: a confetti of might-have-beens.

Hearty: the vice of his eager regard.

Heaven: the place where the dead can continue to hear our excuses.

Hell: the place for those we didn't sufficiently punish on earth.

Helpful: ran away with the wife you were planning to run away from.

Heresy: the negative laid across your positive.

Hermaphrodite: fun alone.

Hesitant: thin.

Hiatus: the hush between allegation and indignation.

History: a catafalque of whines and glitter.

Histrionic: the chicken
 spots the hatchet.

Honest: insufficiently
 tempted.

Holy: the more
 significant other.

Home: place of sighs.

Honorable: the one
 they shoot first.

Hope: a rope ladder
   dangling into the
   smoke.

Hopeless: big waterfall,
   little canoe.

Horror: nothing left to
   distract.

Huckster: convinces the
   satisfied of their
   hunger.

Humane: thinks twice.

Humble: practices being
   short.

Hypocrite: prefers the truth of his cunning.

Idealist: rainbow
 peddler.

Ideologue: robot with
 a smile.

Ill-natured: only sees
 what's absent.

Imagination: escape
 hatch out of any
 second.

Immature: actual tears.

Immediately: the boss's Soon.

Immortal: one's bon mot of the evening just past.

Impatience: the wish to die a little sooner.

Impolitic: the chicken befriends the cook.

Important: wears his necktie to bed.

Imposition: the request that subtracts from your imagined self-
 worth.

Impotent: nubbin redux.

Impresario: the cardinal calls forth the splendiferous dawn.

Imprudent: regales his new bride with tales of his former indiscretions.

Inappreciable: their praise for your job well done.

Incomprehensible: the little bald guy she left you for.

Inconvenient: caught.

Indecisive: a foot on each ice floe.

Indecorous: happy all day, the next day too.

Independent: carved it on his tombstone.

Indigenous: the poor.

Indignation: stepped on your shadow.

Individual: the differentiating belch and squalor.

Ineffable: qualities lacking clear monetary value.

Inequality: a measure of the world's indifference to what you deserve.

Inevitable: that after-dinner story of his near triumphs.

Inexcusable: snags her nose ring in the zipper of his jeans.

Inexhaustible: your helpmate's list of helpful suggestions.

Inexperienced: still at ease with error.

Infatuation: to dabble one's rubber ducky in the high seas of love.

Inflated: books ten rooms at the whorehouse.

Infrastructure: tissue of lies.

Ingratiate: endeavors to be a lullaby in the ears of another.

Innocence: as yet unwrapped.

Innuendo: the noxious seed within the innocuous shell.

Inoffensive: metaphysical ruminant.

Inopportune: the day a bill comes due.

Insanity: reality's fragile option.

Insatiable: makes a soup from the sheets of the night before.

Insidious: dead from the smile up.

Inspirational: the dollar's dog and pony show.

Instinctual: the little spin of the neck as she walks by.

Insufficient: all that happened today.

Insurgent: the mouse slips the trap into your slipper.

Intangible: the vacancy capable of filling a vacuum.

Intellectual: erudition in flight from the abyss.

Intention: fantasy's good idea.

Interminable: the time between the sweet talk and the payoff.

Interrogate: gives a tug at the loose thread of your private life.

Intimacy: four legs, one pair of pants.

Intolerance: becomes impotent; sneers at the eunuch.

Introspective: internal friends.

Invulnerable: pride's swagger.

Isolation: afraid of loving back.

Jabber: continues to argue in the face of your evidence.

Jackal: dogs your footsteps for the secrets you let drop.

Jaded: licked the sheets.

Jail: the martyrdom of aspiration.

Jargon: the encoded banalities of arrogance.

Jaunty: still expects to be thought innocent.

Jealousy: only now he perceives its value.

Jeopardy: your wife examines your credit card receipts.

Jest: view suspiciously unless told by anyone more powerful than yourself.

Jewelry: outer proof of inner value.

Jinx: inimical figment freeing you from admitting your mistake.

Jive: falsehood's tuneful palliative.

Job: the break between TV and sleep.

Joke: air with teeth in it.

Joyous: for now at least, the dark pushed back.

Jubilation: invited as pallbearer at his enemy's funeral.

Juggle: your evasions looping above your defeats.

Judgmental: malice masked as the well-meant.

Judicious: the fox compares the taste of chicken to duck.

Junk: the superseded and formerly loved.

Justifiable: desire decked out as reason.

Juvenile: the joke you don't understand.

Kazoo: your soul's sweetest music in the ears of another.

Keen: still rushes along with his eyes squeezed shut.

Keep: form of rental.

Keepsakes: the junk tossed out by your heirs.

Kennel: favored home for one's conscience.

Key: acquisition's de facto demonstration.

Kindness: sees you briefly as himself.

Kinky: the breaking-in period of any newly found pleasure.

Knack: when you don't wish to ascribe another's success to intellect, hardwork, duplicity or good luck.

Knotty: clarity's infrastructure.

Knowledgeable: venerable opinions.

Known: a fleeting consensus exists.

Laborious: your delight as your boss's wife shows you her daughter's wedding pictures.

Lam: depredation's hurried transparency.

Lamentation: memoir's ubiquitous leitmotiv.

Language: thought's shadow.

Lark: pleasures pursued off one's accustomed path.

Laughter: the grease between you and the world.

Laughter: the sound of the soul chewing.

Lavish: praise given to the undeserving.

Learned: a platitude for every occasion.

Lechery: the genitals' version of collecting stamps.

Leer: his lips duplicate his belly's curve.

Legal: the uninspired course.

Legend: the cradle of memoir.

Legitimate: falsehood with a pedigree.

Leisure: your boss explains the bright side of being fired.

Leitmotiv: the story of his near successes.

Levity: best time to ask for a loan.

Libel: someone calling you
what you secretly call
yourself.

Libido: the body's happy
charioteer.

Library: warehouse for
alternative truths.

License: the permission not to
ask permission.

Life: your stretch of river.

Lifelike: one's former spouse.

Literate: half a dozen
memorized quotations
strategically placed.

Litigate: to bully with paper.

Lobotomy: on most people the scars don't show.

Loneliness: unwatered soul.

Long-winded: the other point of view.

Loot: what it boils down to.

Love: where I erase myself.

Loyal: still dickering with your enemies.

Lucky: how else can you explain his success?

Lycanthropy: the essential condition.

Lyricism: the heart's burnished spring wound tight.

Madden: refuses to withhold advice.

Magnanimous: when you are down, he kicks you only a little.

Malice: the wish to have others feel as badly as you do.

Mammary: tit with a higher level of taboo.

Manipulate: to assist another along the wiser path.

Manuscript: fetal tissue.

Martyr: prefers the fame of his defeats.

Marxist: offers your socks to others.

Mascot: significant dummy.

Masculine: likes trucks.

Maudlin: up to his neck in might-have-beens.

Meddlesome: keeps asking how you earned it.

Mediocre: destined for public office.

Mediocrity: seeks to muzzle.

Meditation: the worrying that makes you feel better about worrying.

Meek: keeps the knife behind his back.

Melancholy: inner map full of culs-de-sac.

Mellow: vigorously slothful.

Melodious: the tweedle of his accomplishments in his inner ear.

Melodramatic: he forgot her mother's birthday.

Memory: sawdust heaped outside a mill.

Menace: fifteen passing for eighteen.

Menagerie: life at the office.

Menial: the dog's dog.

Merchandise: keepsakes in utero.

Meticulous: life in little bites.

Minion: the one who you let keep the change.

Mirror: always kisses back.

Misanthrope: one truth too many.

Mitigating: white-collar excuses.

Moderation: the course we urge on others.

Modesty: so you can take a larger helping later on.

Modish: adds a feather.

Money: death's fur coat.

Music: the conviction of order.

Mystery: what language seeks to conceal.

Nag: the petitioner's debauch.

Naïve: what innocence calls ignorance.

Naked: fashion's raw material.

Name: abstract apparel.

Narcissism: surrendering to the one you can always trust.

Narcissist: the mirror's confidant.

Narration: the shuffle between Why and If.

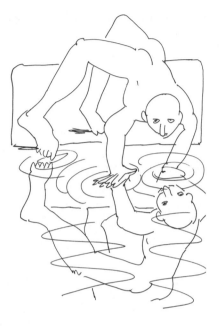

Narrative: two or more complaints in a row.

Narrow-minded: noun-bound.

Nationalism: a chip on the border.

Nauseated: proactive indignation.

Necessity: appetite's lieutenant.

Necktie: money's leash.

Nerve: a crisis of caution.

Nervousness: the imagination's struggle with consequence.

Nihilist: left the fire sale empty-handed.

Nitpick: to trifle with your truth.

Nocturne: the music by which the owl fattens.

Noir: dangles his heart from a toothpick.

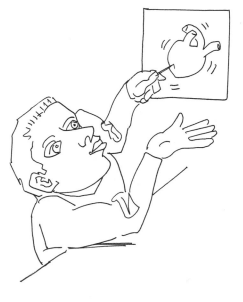

Normal: mediocrity's sop.

Nostalgia: recollection's celestial attraction.

Nothingness: the echo's substantiality.

Noun: the attempt to give shape to the ephemeral.

Nymphet: green tomato.

Oafish: plants his big feet across your truth.

Objectivity: the robot's mocking grin.

Oblivion: freedom from the oughts and might-have-beens.

Obnoxious: feels certain you want his advice.

Obscenity: to remain indifferent.

Obsequious: offers himself as the butter for your bread.

Obsolete: youthful ambitions.

Opinions: a blind man's candles.

Opportunity: rainy day and your boss forgot his umbrella.

Oppressed: resentments exceed expectations.

Options: credible fantasies.

Ordinary: worse than failure.

Orgasm: the rainbow over the dog bed.

Ornament: the image his vanity regards in the mirror.

Ostentatious: don't you kick a mule to get its attention?

Overpraise: not, in your case, yet.

Over-the-hill: can't strike back.

Ownership: a kiss of longer duration.

Pain: mortality's souvenir.

Passive: loiters at the crossroads of patience and sleep.

Pathetic: blameless life, apologizes nonetheless.

Patience: the open door that allows the world to enter.

Peace: to be concerned no longer.

Persecute: to make your name a thorn in his tongue.

Pessimist: lacks the gift of self-deception.

Pet: the creature that always listens.

Philosopher: complains about tomorrow the day before.

Philosophy: what he calls his bad ideas.

Pimp: no ideas but in things.

Plausible: the stupid ideas of the powerful.

Pleasure: the air knit by music.

Pluralistic: two for me, one for you.

Pompous: borne up by the breathy exhalations of his self-regard.

Pragmatist: makes beauty ride in back.

Prankster: jiggles your pulpit.

Precious: those secret self-directed sweet nothings.

Prejudice: hostility directed at another for not being one's self.

Preoccupied: two or more worries occupying the same space at the same time.

Prepubescent: the truth comes in whispers.

Present moment: the space through which chance passes to become destiny.

Prevaricate: hesitating over the lie that suits you best.

Preventable: what they say later.

Pride: a palace invisible to others.

Priggish: frowns upon the fucking of others.

Primitive: never gets your jokes.

Principled: timid.

Principles: complaints in a three-piece suit.

Procreate: to make a little stranger to teach your side of the story.

Professor: grades others on his ignorance.

Promiscuity: two pricks, one for resting up.

Proof: your vast coup de grâce or the peevish quibbling of a sore loser.

Property: the glue joining the feathers of which you are composed.

Prosaic: last year's ideas today.

Proverbial: their favorite clichés.

Provincial: envies clerks; takes long naps.

Prudence: says no before it's offered.

Pusillanimous: clears his throat, won't speak.

Quaint: on bended knee.

Qualifier: pre-first-date blood test.

Quality: underserved if not one's own.

Qualms: never heeded in time.

Quantify: attempt to remove the mystery.

Quantum Jump: car coming.

Quarrel: the denouement of another's inflexibility.

Quarrelsome: would have you bear the burden of his disappointment.

Quarry: first date.

Quasi: the nuance explaining another's talent.

Quaver: melodic shading to enhance any request.

Quest: the pursuit of surfeit.

Question: treat with suspicion.

Questioning: suggests an unsteady temper.

Quibble: quarrel's doorstep.

Quick: death no closer
    yet.

Quickie: fleshes out a
    quiet moment.

Quip: the distillation of
    your critic's marshaled
    facts.

Quirk: a yet-to-be-applied
    ability.

Quixotic: another's raison
    d'être.

Quiz: seemingly affable,
    your interrogators have
    several questions.

Quotable: those flattering
    sweet nothings.

Rabble: bellies on the loose.

Raffish: cocks his hat and thinks himself dancing.

Rampage: the tongue abandons consequence.

Random: the inopportune disruptor of the predestined.

Rascal: two jokes and a hand on your wallet.

Ravage: weasels doing weasel work.

Rebel: sheep in wolf's clothing.

Rebut: befriends your inconsistencies.

Received Ideas: the tried and true.

Reconciliation: salt and sugar in the same shaker.

Regret: sorry he didn't take seconds.

Rehabilitate: the cat hangs a bell from its collar.

Relevant: one's personal digression.

Reminiscence: to change the never-to-be-imagined to the never-doubted.

Rendezvous: two crows share a dead squirrel.

Resentment: pain's echo.

Responsible: bullied by bankers.

Résumé: plot-driven, nonnarrative fiction.

Retirement: no-man's-land.

Revelation: the bursting forth of second thoughts.

Revenge: when you can't win.

Revisionism: the step before memoir.

Risk: knits his own condoms.

Ritual: the habit you can't break.

Romance: procreation's bob and whistle.

Rotten: the crow calls it cooked.

Routine: one more virgin; one more broken heart.

Ruin: mouse snuck the cat's fishy.

Ruse: you must show me your work.

Ruthless: deaf to your excuses.

Sabotage: tosses another woman's panties under your wife's side of the bed.

Safety: nothing left to surrender.

Sanity: save a bit for when the party stops.

Sarcasm: the untuned string on consolation's violin.

Satisfied: ask for another taste just to make sure.

Scam: former sure thing.

Scandal: the dog that always creeps home.

Scorn: to shrink the one who looms large in the mind.

Scribbler: uses a pen to polish his excuses.

Self: smoke and cobweb infrastructure.

Self-analysis: blind man drawing a dog.

Self-criticism: worth praising at dinner parties.

Self-deception: the monkey writes another sonnet and sighs.

Self-hatred: an excess of self-love.

Self-indulgent: his wallet wants him to be happy.

Selfish: belly knows best.

Self-pity: the embrace that matters most.

Sexuality: makes up for having nothing to say.

Shebang (whole): three rabbits in each claw.

Shrewd: the wolf goes gobble, gobble.

Silence: no moon and the owl glides over the meadow.

Silly: fattens his inner child.

Simulacrum: the self he sends out to misbehave.

Skulk: attentive to your inattention.

Slander: words in black gloves.

Sleep: practicing to get it right.

Sloth: life in the conditional mode.

Smidgen: humility's portion.

Sneer: the teeth must find something funny.

Snub: mistook you for air.

Solitude: nothing to make an echo.

Soon: the last guarantee to
lose its luster.

Sophistication: cynicism
tinseled with charm.

Soulful: the fox sings at the
chicken's funeral.

Souvenir: scarlike.

Sparse: the gratitude for all
that good advice.

Spasm: after the orchids and champagne.

Specter: the self that wakes you to remember.

Spendthrift: gave his gift to little songs.

Spiritual: fucks them, then writes the poem.

Spite: a tooth in every kiss.

Splurge: to validate oneself through excess.

Squabble: two salesmen, one cell phone.

Stacked: would be a fool not to look.

Standard Bearer: to be the feather in another's cap.

Stench: the residue of beauty.

Stodgy: lies in his coffin for fun.

Stooge: proud to carry the bully's brass knuckles.

Strange: frontier between ignorance and knowledge.

Strategy: two weasels; three rabbit holes.

Strident: the sum of all complaint.

Structure: the picket fence between party and paycheck.

Stubborn: forges an anchor from his pride.

Student: still making up his mind.

Studious: the pickpocket selects the crowd as text.

Stupefy: tells you again about his operation.

Subconscious: éminence grise.

Success: the meal digested, the turd passed.

Sucker: thought to get the dream cheap.

Sufficiency: an existential condition experienced by others.

Sugar: the tongue's philosophy.

Suicide: indecorous withdrawal.

Superficial: behind his smile—arid fields, a dog barking.

Superfluous: to die and shit one's pants as well.

Supremacist: auto-coronated.

Surly: hurt pride's chain-link fence.

Surveillance: the attention that doesn't flatter.

Suspense: your head on the block, the executioner starts to sneeze.

Swank: pig in a frock coat.

Sycophant: shadow licker.

Symbiosis: I like your poems, too.

Symbol: whatever one doesn't understand.

Synopsis: he danced; he died.

Taboo: the secret self's exquisite denials.

Taciturn: prefers his second thoughts.

Tact: falsehood's charming décolletage.

Talent: a pair of deuces.

Talk: soul rattle.

Tantrum: useful when losing an argument.

Taste: what he calls his ignorance.

Tears: heart sweat.

Tears: the body's additional two cents.

Temptation: the belief that something ahead makes up for something behind.

Tender: to touch another as yourself.

Tenderness: takes out his dentures before kissing.

Tenure: the excuse to strip off your falsies and corset.

Terrible: time's careless ravaging of one's options.

Testimonial: brags about his wife's virtue to the whore.

Text: is to poem what biped is to sexpot.

Theft: socialized entropy.

Theory: rubber ice pick chipping at the dark.

Thespian: lies well.

Thing: the rabbit hears the rush of wings.

Think: fingers
disturbing whole
villages of lice.

Threaten: to impose
the gift of humility.

Thrifty: drops a smile
in the beggar's tin
cup.

Time: the ineffable
effability.

Tit: little pick-me-up.

Today: infant history.

Toil: was it good for you, too?

Tolerant: easily unthreatened.

Tomb: dust factory.

Topical: the tinseled apparency.

Topless: the sudden revelation of opportunities lost.

Torrid: the heart strikes a match.

Tourist: noncommittal.

Tradition: error's cherished accumulation.

Tragedy: the boss spilled his soup.

Tranquillity: ask the cow.

Trash: chattels' kingdom come.

Treachery: sooner or later.

Trickery: beneath the hoopla of his genius.

Trivialize: to nullify nonviolently.

Truth: unlit candle.

Truth: the province of the loud.

Truth: a lie incognito.

Turgid: the bear explains Nietzsche.

Turmoil: six tits; two hands.

Twaddle: earnestness on bended knee.

Tyranny: curbs the riffraff.

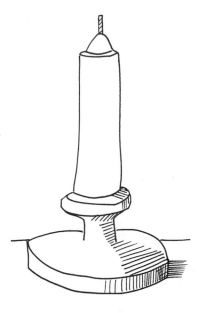

Ubiquitous: the temptations you can barely resist.

Uglier: the children of your friends.

Ugliness: anything looked at too briefly or too long.

Ulterior: the smile's smile.

Ultimatum: no grovel, no prize.

Umbrage: indignation's doorbell.

Unanimous: must have written a lot of checks.

Unapproachable: cute nun.

Unavailing: the chicken offers the fox an egg.

Unbiased: omnivore.

Uncertain: pretty girl, old condom.

Uncivilized: unappreciative of your point of view.

Unclassifiable: your enemies' iniquities.

Unconditional: postponed conditions.

Unconscious: removes her clothes, keeps his nose in a book.

Unctuous: greasy hands.

Undaunted: too proud to call it stubborn.

Underhanded: nonlitigious.

Unfair: the slipping away of the immense unoffered largesse.

Unified: his enemies set aside their differences.

Unimaginable: somebody already has.

Unique: only when alone.

Unmanned: her little
   chuckle when he drops
   his shorts.

Unnatural: wins a prize,
   doesn't brag.

Unreal: one's assumptions
   about what is real.

Unruly: the belly's bill of
   rights.

Unworldly: no cell phone.

Urgent: tenth in line for
   the toilet.

Utopian: no dream too
   big.

Vain: can't see past the lipstick on the mirror.

Validate: buys himself what he can't afford.

Vamp: salt dressed as sugar.

Vanity: what you feed first.

Vapid: measures his passion with teaspoons.

Venal: fox-hearted.

Vendetta: resentment ennobled.

Venereal: everything gone to waist.

Vengeful: because you didn't care enough.

Veracity: what he calls his tactlessness.

Verbose: for you alone his candied lexicon.

Versify: banality tortured into song.

Victim: pre-beef.

Vigilante: truth ad hoc.

Vindication: gold watch and a handshake too.

Vindictive: one crime, two punishments.

Virile: multi-scrotumed.

Virtuous: belly must be full.

Vitality: double-hearted.

Void: non-you.

Voluptuary: the fox in his cloak of iridescent feathers.

Vulgar: fell asleep over your book.

Vulture: envy's beak in the belly of contentment.

Wag: chuckle-hearted.

Waif: unembraced.

Wander: no one waiting.

Wastrel: sieve-fingered.

Wealth: the trouble
    that makes it better.

Weapon: resentments
    rigidified.

Well-meaning: offers to
    teach your wife a
    trick or two.

Whisper: ulteriorese.

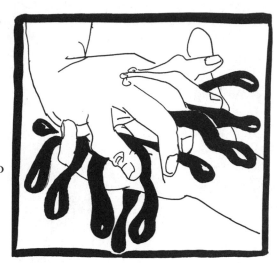

Wholesome: as yet unpackaged.

Wild: civilization's discontents.

Wilderness: the land beyond the paycheck.

Wiles: the fox rents a wheelchair.

Winner: future loser.

Wisdom: able to say no in time.

Wish: when now isn't enough.

Wit: the brain's guffaw.

Wolfish: market driven.

Womanize: gets caught looking.

Word: brain drop.

Worry: night gristle.

Worship: hankers upward.

Worship: the view from beneath the money tree.

Wronged: she even took the dog.

X: the excuses he will offer once he finds them.

Xanthic: apparent coward.

Xanthippe: heard one bromide too many.

X Chromosome: proto-Cleopatra.

Xenogenetic: adolescent.

Xenophobe: barbed-wire
  enthusiast.

Xenophobic: at night he
  hears the shadows
  complain.

Xerophilous: critical
  theorist.

X-rated: excessively
  educational.

Xyloid: tenured.

Yawn: dreamspeak.

Y Chromosome: half in the bag.

Year: resentment's sausage link.

Yearning: solutions on the horizon.

Yen: belly itch.

Yesterday: the Almost preceding today's Not Quite.

Yielding: offer her another chocolate.

Yokel: offers no sport.

Yonder: blue but not sad.

You: proof of not me.

Your imperfections: what makes the water sparkle at sunset.

Youth: ignorance in a gift box.

Youthful Ambitions: the creatures sighing beneath his bed at night.

Yowl: the agony of song.

Yowl: the magnificat of one's personal misadventures.

Zany: the yet to be accepted by common consensus.

Zap: big tits at the beach.

Zeal: untroubled by pros and cons.

Zealot: no cost too high.

Zealous: fifty-second minutes.

Zeitgeist: takes the blame for whatever you choose not to blame.

Zephyr: rich man's fart.

Zero: waits while all the rest is lost.

Zest: infatuation's regardlessness.

Zilch: the overreacher's recompense.

ACKNOWLEDGMENTS

Many thanks are due to the editors of the following publications in which this work first appeared.

Prose Poems

American Poetry Review: (A love of music); (Although in the thick of a journey); (At times it was in French or pages were missing); (At times he tried to locate the moment of change); (For years he thought madness must be peaceful); (Friends with whom he had quarreled); (Harsh words, dismissive gestures); (He felt best moving between two points); (He grew fond of his uncertainties); (He had spent his youth); (He loved his joy); (He loved the general over the particular); (His definition of beauty); (In some dreams he could run); (Of course he saw that his dislike of received ideas); (Say that each word is a board); (That day he and the woman spent hours on horseback); (The choices were between his life and his art); (When he felt most loved); (When he was making love).

The Gettysburg Review: (A Bach partita or one of the Goldberg Variations); (How he nurtured his cynicism); (In the beginning, he was like a crowd); (When the leaves fell and the October wind shook the trees).

The Harvard Review: (Birdsong, sunsets); (For one it was the wish to be loved); (He knew it was foolish); (Those brick walls).

Poetry: (Friends of his youth, friends of his prime); (He knew his vulnerabilities); (His failures—could he blame them on time?); (His life was the practice of forming a single sentence); (It was the lack of certainty that disturbed him); (Over a cup of coffee or sitting on a park bench); (Over here he made a pile); (Such days as these); (Such pleasures he had taken in books); (The more he considered his death); (To stand on a high place).

Southern Review: (His want formed a craving never satisfied); (Often, in dreams, he moved through a city); (The pleasure of creating something); (You take a train through a foreign country).

Virginia Quarterly Review: (At the ocean he studied the waves); (He felt bullied by his possessions); (Sometimes confusion was a veil across his eyes); (Occasionally and for what seemed no reason); (The clouds above the mountains).

A number of the considerations and definitions appeared in *The Harvard Review, Many Mountains Moving,* and *Poetry.*

ABOUT THE AUTHOR

Stephen Dobyns has published ten prior books of poetry and twenty novels, including ten mystery novels set in Saratoga Springs. His collection of essays on poetry, *Best Words, Best Order*, appeared in 1996. His first book of poems, *Concurring Beasts*, was the Lamont Poetry Selection for 1972 of the Academy of American Poets. *Black Dog, Red Dog* was a winner in the National Poetry Series. *Cemetery Nights* won the Poetry Society of America's Melville Cane Award in 1987. Dobyns has received a Guggenheim and three fellowships from the National Endowment of the Arts. His most recent book of poetry is *Pallbearers Envying the One Who Rides* (1999). His most recent book of fiction is a collection of stories, *Eating Naked* (2000). Dobyns lives with his family near Boston. He teaches in the MFA program at Sarah Lawrence College.

HOWIE MICHELS (SELF)

ABOUT THE ILLUSTRATOR

Howie Michels lives and works in New York City and upstate New York.

PENGUIN POETS